(Paperback) 979-8-89269-921-1

(Ebook) 979-8-89269-922-8

Disclaimer: This is a work of fiction. Any resemblance to actual events or persons, living or dead, is entirely coincidental.

Editing by Book Baby

Illustrated by Karinadewi Comic's

Self- Publish by Shareka Thomas

What is *Kwanzaa*?

Kwanzaa is a relatively new holiday. African American scholar, professor, and activist Maulana Karenga created *Kwanzaa* in the 1960s when he was 25 years old. In doing so, he combined elements from various African harvest celebrations to highlight the values and strength of the African American community, like the struggle for self-determination, equality, and justice. In a 2008 newspaper interview, Karenga said he created the holiday to "give Blacks an opportunity to celebrate themselves and their history."

Kwanzaa is a celebration of African heritage and Black culture, and it's also meant to be a counter to holidays that center mainstream culture and consumerism. Though it's most observed in the United States, people in the African diaspora celebrate *Kwanzaa* in other parts of the world, too. According to a 2012 study, approximately 4 percent of Americans reported celebrating *Kwanzaa*—which would represent more than 12.5 million people.

The seven principles of *Kwanzaa*

The seven-day holiday is defined by the seven principles (or *Nguzu Saba*) of *Kwanzaa*, which are typically referenced by their Swahili word. Each principle has a day devoted to it and to discussion about what it represents. The seven principles are:

- Umoja (unity)
- Kujichagulia (self-determination)
- Ujima (collective work and responsibility)
- Ujamaa (cooperative economics)
- Nia (purpose)
- Kuumba (creativity)
- Imani (faith)

Principles of Kwanzaa
Umoja
Unity
Kujichagulia
Self-Determination
Ujima
Collective Work
Ujamaa
Cooperative Economics
Nia
Purpose
Kuumba
Creativity
Imani
Faith

"I don't think there will ever be a time when the principles of Kwanzaa will not be important or timely. It's a great time for reflection and now more than ever our country needs to be reminded of unity."

— *Kellie Carter Jackson*

Kwanzaa Family Values

Learning about Kwanzaa has never been fun until now!

"Wake up my son, it's training day!" Pride's parents said overjoyed with excitement. "Five more minutes please, sleep was rough last night for me; I was too excited about today," Pride could barely keep his eyes open.

"Well Mr. Sleepyhead, you have four minutes left," Pride's mother joked with him as she and his father left his room.

"Joy, I can't believe that it's finally time to introduce Pride to our family's tradition! This year flew by so fast after having my Pride and Joy," Mr. Kwanzaa giggled. "I remember like it was yesterday when my parents enlightened me about our tradition and values," Pride's father reminisced.

"I remember too," Joy smiled thinking of her mother's lovely voice. "Mom loved music so much that she could make a song out of anything," Pride parents both laughed. "I guess I should ask you instead of assuming, so which way will we be teaching junior?" Mrs. Kwanzaa asked Mr. Kwanzaa.

"Well, my dear that's a good question. You were taught the tradition through melody and to look at the tradition from building a strong foundation for your community aspect; my parents taught me to create more business opportunities using these principles," Mr. Kwanzaa replied.

"How about we try and incorporate both, so that way he has options someday for his little ones?" Mrs. Kwanzaa suggested. "Sounds fair," replied Mr. Kwanzaa, pleased with the agreement. "Good morning mom and dad," Pride yawned, still very sleepy. "Let's get this party started." Pride thought to himself, I've been waiting on this moment all my life. "Good morning my sunshine, your father and I are very excited about today as well," Mrs. Kwanzaa smiled at her boys.

"So, your mom and I have decided that we will both teach you the ways that our parents taught us, one being a melody that you can sing to your family someday and one being a way to build a stable business to provide for your family," Mr. Kwanzaa explained.

"First things first son, your name is Pride, but do you know what you are called and what your function or purpose is during this wonderful time of the year?" Mr. Kwanzaa was ready to teach. "Well, I'm not sure what to call myself, but I know my job during this season is to hold I think seven candles," Pride answered to the best of his ability.

"Very well son" Mrs. Kwanzaa was pleased with his observation. "We are called Kinaras; we are special candleholders that are used during the Kwanzaa celebration. The seven candles that you speak of honors different principles of African culture. These principles are believed to have been the key to building strong, productive families and communities in Africa," Mr. Kwanzaa said proudly.

"The seven candles that are placed on you have a special order starting from left to right. The first three candles are red, then you have your center candle which is black, and the last three are green," Mrs.Kwanzaa added.

"Each color symbolizes something different; the black candle is for the people, the red candle is for their struggle, and the green candle is for future hope. It's such a secret celebration that even lighting the candle has a special order," Mr. Kwanzaa said. "This is a lot of information. How did you obtain all these as kids?" Pride was feeling overwhelmed. "Baby boy, we are just scratching the surface, my father made me take notes, and your mother learned by song, maybe you should take notes, son. Go ahead and grab some supplies," Mr. Kwanzaa instructed.

"Okay dad, you can continue" Pride listened carefully." Like I was saying, it's such a secret celebration that even lighting the candle has a special order. This celebration starts the day after Christmas and ends on New Year's Day.

The black candle is the first to be lit on the first day, then on the second day, the red candle near the black is to be lit, then on the third day the first green candle near the black one is to be lit. On the fourth day, you light the next red candle near the black one, and you keep switching sides every day until New Year's." Mr. Kwanzaa took a deep breath.

"All of the candles have unique names and special meaning behind them! Are you ready to sing, son? Because I need you to repeat after me as I teach you the names and meanings," Mrs.Kwanzaa cleared her throat, ready for the duet with her son. "Ready as I can be mom, "Pride was so excited about the song. "Sounds good, repeat after me," Mrs. Kwanzaa began.

"I said umoja (oo-MOH-ja)," Mrs.Kwanzaa pointed at Pride. "I said umoja" Pride repeated. "It means unity," "it means unity." "Unity is strength...when there is teamwork and collaboration, wonderful things can be achieved. "Building a community that holds together is very important; you can also use this to build a successful business," Mr. Kwanzaa added.

"I said kujichagulia (koo-jee-cha-goo-LEE-yah)," "kujichagulia." "It means self-determination," "it means self-determination." "Always speak up for yourself and make choices that benefit everyone, not just yourself. Remember son, our deeds determine us, as much as we determine our deeds. "The difference between the impossible and the possible lies in a person's determination," Mr. Kwanzaa added.

"I said ujima (oo-JEE-mah)," "I said ujima." "It means collective work and responsibility," "it means collective work and responsibility." "Helping others is the way to helping ourselves, a kind gesture can reach a wound that only compassion can heal." We rise by lifting others," Mr.Kwanzaa was on a roll.

"I said ujamaa (oo-JAH-ma)," "I said ujamaa." "It means cooperative economics," "it means cooperative economics." "By building your own businesses, you control the economics of your own community. Life is a boomerang; what you give is what you get back in return. Always give back to make this a better place," Mr.Kwanzaa preached.

"I said nia (nee-AH)," "I said nia." "It means a sense of purpose," "it means a sense of purpose." "Set goals that will benefit you and the community, you were put on earth to achieve your greatest self. You are not here on earth to merely survive; you were created to THRIVE. You were born to make a dramatic difference," Mr. Kwanzaa flexed his muscles.

"I said kuumba (koo-OOM-bah)," "I said kuumba." "It means creativity," "it means creativity.""Make the community better and more beautiful, some people look for a beautiful place, and others make a beautiful place," Mr. Kwanzaa expressed.

"My favorite one, I said imani (ee-MAH-nee)," "I said imani." "It means faith," "it means faith." "Always believe that a better world can be created for communities, now and in the future; faith is seeing light with you heart when all your eye see is darkness," Mr. Kwanzaa clapped.

"And that's a wrap!" Mrs. Kwanzaa was done with all seven candles, next season your father and I will watch you lead the celebration. I am so proud of you, baby; I'm sure you will do well," Mrs. Kwanzaa hugged Pride. "That was fun, mom and dad; let's do it again," Pride wasn't ready for it to end.

"Just study those notes, and you'll be fine," Mr. Kwanzaa stated. "It's almost time to light the first candle; pop quiz really quick before we start: What candle do you light first, son?" Mrs. Kwanzaa questioned Pride. "The black candle ujamaa! Did I get it right, mom? Did I get it right?" "You sure did! Great job, son, now let's get this party started in your voice." The entire family laughed as they headed to the table to stand tall and strong through the celebration of Kwanzaa.

Word Search

```
O F A I T H I J P N Z N A W I R R U
S E L F D E T E R M I N A T I O N J
Q K L C R E A T I V I T Y Y S B T S
U U D U J A M A A W T H Z M W X S M
J U B J W U M O J A W Q S I C J N Q
I M M V U Z L V J Q W D M C I Z U W
M B I M A N I D E Y W X J N I A I N
A A X I S K U J I C H A G U L I A B
N I G X V B N Y O P U R P O S E S W
A A P U N I T Y C Z J Z B S L G W E
F O R E S P O N S I B I L I T Y K V
G C O L L E C T I V E W O R K Q T M
```

Find the following words in the puzzle.
Words are hidden → ↓ and ↘ .

COLLECTIVE WORK	KUUMBA	UJAMAA
CREATIVITY	NIA	UJIMA
FAITH	PURPOSE	UMOJA
IMANI	RESPONSIBILITY	UNITY
KUJICHAGULIA	SELF-DETERMINATION	

https://www.ohmydots.com

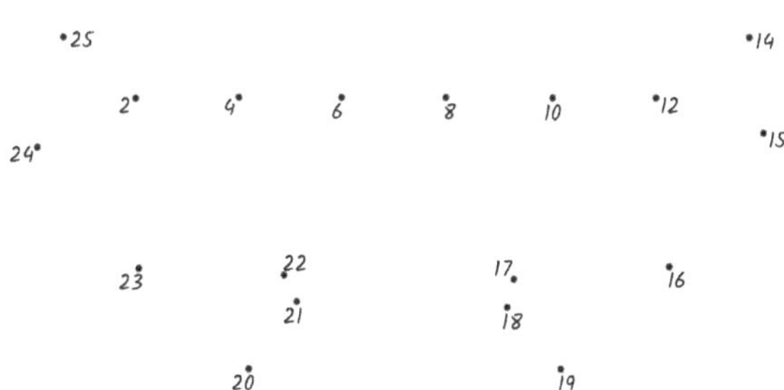

Connect the dots have fun!!!!

Pop Quiz

1. Where are the candles placed during Kwanzaa?

    A. Kinara

    B. A Candelaburm

    C. Chamberstick

    D. A Menorah

2. Which value is not one of the values recognized during Kwanzaa?

    A. Courage

    B. Creativity

    C. Collective Work

    D. Cooperative Economics

3. When does Kwanzaa begin?

    A. January 1st

    B. December 20th

    C. December 26th

    D. It Constantly Changes

4. What does Kwanzaa celebrate?

A. American Culture

B. European Culture

C. African Culture

D. Asian Culture

5. Which colors are used to celebrate Kwanzaa?

A. Red, Green and Black

B. Red, Green and White

C. Black, Green and Yellow

D. Red, Black, Yellow

6. How many red candles are present during Kwanzaa?

A. 5 Red Candles

B. 1 Red Candles

C. 7 Red Candles

D. 3 Red Candles

Answer

1. A 2.D 3.C 4.C 5.A

Mindset Fresh Book Collection

This wonderful book collection is available in two formats. Ebook (Amazon Kindle) paperback in over 450 book retailers, bookstores, and libraries all over the US and other territories, so make sure you visit your nearby bookstore in person or shop online.

Litty & The Giant
Print **ISBN** 978-1-63848-383-0
Ebook **ISBN** 978-1-63877-969-8

Blue & Wormy Self-Love Stroll to School
Print **ISBN** 978-1-0879-8363-9
Ebook **ISBN** 978-1-0879-8360-8

My Favorite Apple Tree
Print **ISBN** 979-8-88589-637-5
Ebook **ISBN** 979-8-88589-638-2

On My Journey 2 Greatness
Print **ISBN** 978-1-63848-386-1
Ebook **ISBN** 978-1-63901-912-0

Mindset Fresh 31 Day Reflection Journal
Print **ISBN** 978-1-the 63877-967-1
Ebook **ISBN** 978-1-63877-969-8

Mindset Fresh Kid's Reflection Journal
Print **ISBN** 978-1-63877-955-1
Ebook **ISBN** 978-1-63877-956-8

My Millionaire Routine
Print **ISBN** 978--8-88796-879-7
Ebook **ISBN** 978-8-88796-870-4

Broken Promise
Print **ISBN** 979-8-89238-117-8
Ebook **ISBN** 979-8-89238-119-2

About Author

Shareka Thomas challenges people of all ages to live out their own "Phenomenal Self". Her motivation comes from childhood experiences, as there were times where she struggled with self-doubt, fear, and adversity. Over the years she has overcome those barriers through prayer, listening to motivational speakers, changing her perspective, facing her fears, and speaking nothing but positivity into her life existence.

She loves to share her story and encourage others to discover their superpower and climb endless stairs of possibilities. She believes that if you walk by faith and not by sight nothing is impossible. If you can dream it, you can achieve it.